I Would Have Left You Everything

Charlotte Lit Press
Charlotte Center for Literary Arts, Inc.
PO Box 18607
Charlotte, NC 28218
charlottelit.org/press

Cover art by Suzanne Sbarge
Author photo by Wan Chih Sbarge

ISBN: 978-1-960558-04-6

PROUD MEMBER

[clmp]

COMMUNITY OF LITERARY MAGAZINES & PRESSES
WWW.CLMP.ORG

I Would Have Left You Everything

Eric Sbarge

Charlotte Center for Literary Arts, Inc.
Charlotte, North Carolina
charlottelit.org

To my late parents, who lovingly read books to me when I was young, and read me the riot act as I got older.

Contents

Covenants

Propped up against my mailbox
in jeans and a flannel shirt that I never
would have chosen to wear
on such a hot day
I'm passed by neighbors
pushing baby strollers
or pumping arms with hand weights
and one or two nod or say hello

but most take a wide berth
staring or trying
not to stare
until finally one stops and rings
the doorbell which my wife answers
and the concerned neighbor says
your husband doesn't look well
and isn't moving

to which she replies
that's because he's dead
and if I could I would high-five her
for following through on
her promise not
to cremate me right away
but instead place me out
by the mailbox for a day or two

as a polite way of voicing
one final fuck you
to our neighborhood HOA
with their life-draining covenants
and officious warnings
about what you can and cannot
display in front of your
own home.

Hiding Something

If you have a large wad of cash
you're asked to hide it
deep in your pockets

ostensibly for safety or maybe
so the cashless won't feel demoralized
by their dearth.

Those with a vagina or a penis
are asked to please cover it
in public, perhaps

not to offend or maybe not to dishearten
the unfortunate few who must
go without.

I would like to go on, but the bull frogs
in the pond next door are loudly and relentlessly
croaking one croak after another,

their frog parts naked
and greenbacks fully exposed.
I don't know what they're trying to hide.

Forgiveness

A small bird flies against your window
and falls to the ground, hobbled.
You're tempted to run to it and shit
on its head or shoulders but your mantra
there is no revenge so complete as forgiveness
prompts you to instead place the bird
in a box on a soft new towel.

Online you learn that injured birds
that haven't flown within two hours
should be taken to a licensed bird rehabilitator
so you spend half the afternoon looking
for one (imagine the karma of taking a bird
to an unlicensed one) and the other half driving it there.
Upon arrival you peer into the box
and find it lying on its back
which you presume is a bird's way
of flipping you the bird without fingers—
but why? Doesn't it realize
you're trying to help it even though
its kind have ruined your kind's hats
and hairdos and suits and sweaters forever?

You turn the bird back over and discover
cream-colored shit all over your new towel
but your forgiveness holds
and you congratulate the rehabilitator
for passing her licensing test and she looks
at you quizzically as she carries the bird away.

Months later at a new restaurant
you walk right into a very clean glass door
and as you rub your forehead
you begin to understand.

Small Hinges Swing Big Doors

has been repeated for centuries by countless
Chinese characters
from sages to scholars to big sisters
and window and door installers—
evoking images of red front doors for good luck
weathered gray doors for the downtrodden
and impenetrable doors to the hearts
of the heartbroken.

I open my shower door and step in, grateful
for the small things in life—
warm showers on cool mornings, cool showers
on warm mornings. Why, I wonder, would a benevolent
God grant us icy-cold streams on icy-cold days
or hot and steamy swimming holes
on hot and steamy days?

The scent of lather from the new bottle of soap
my Taiwan-born wife special-ordered from Hong Kong
breaks my ruminations—a soap whose perfect fragrance
is completely foreign to me, inscrutable and unknown
like the Chinese characters on the bottle
that I cannot read.

Something about that magical scent makes my thoughts
of the world and God's shortcomings bind
with the creamy lather and run down my body
through the drain deep into the earth below,
leaving only a Zen state of tranquility.

I begin to see why the Chinese
don't need to speak much of God,
that small bottle of soap
having swung open by another few degrees
the enormous gates of heaven.

Poem Love Mandarin

wife my for love of Out
Taiwan in raised was who
Mandarin speak they where
written traditionally was which
lines vertical in left to right from
.left to right from poem this writing I'm

lines vertical in this write to have don't I
we married got we when since however
equally cultures our share to agreed
in marriage of sake the for and
meet always to general
.way half other each

A Bothersome Foot

I tell my podiatrist who happens to be my daughter
that my foot's been hurting when I walk.
She examines it carefully and gives me her diagnosis—
I'm tying my shoes too tightly.
I remind her that I've been tying my own shoes
for over fifty years so I know how to tie shoes
but she shrugs and says try tying them
looser for a few days and see what happens.
I follow her instructions with reluctance
and after just two days the pain is completely gone
which is probably a coincidence but either way
I volunteer that since patients pay her good money
for their exams she might sound more professional
if she'd use the Latin term for tie your shoes looser
which to save her time I have already looked up
on Google and while I'm sure I mispronounce
ligabis calceamenta tua laxiora she says she will
take my suggestion under consideration
then adds that since she's treating me pro bono
I could at least make a little bit of effort to acknowledge
her hard-earned knowledge and expertise.
I compliment her on the astounding erudition
she exhibited by correctly using the Latin phrase pro bono
which prompts her to share a different Latin phrase
that she learned in podiatry school—*me vexat pede*—
which she explains translates literally as a bothersome foot
but in common usage refers to a trivial person
who's a complete pain in the ass.
Having earned the last word as she always does
she impels me to walk away, my respect and admiration
and deep love for her adding an extra
spring to my step.

The Farmer's Daughter

When your car breaks down
and the farmer says you can
spend the night
don't expect to be frolicking in the hay
with his daughter.

Today's farmer's daughter is no joke—
she may have the voluptuous body
of your adolescent dreams, but you'll
never know since she's away at Stanford
earning her Ph.D. in engineering.

You'll be stuck sitting on the sofa
through the wee hours
sipping orange soda pop with her dad
learning more than you ever wanted to know
about combine harvesters.

Nude at the Stove

I'm not fooled by Vallotton's
Nude at the Stove—
that pensive beauty will never
glance my way
and that stove will remain
cold as stone in winter.

You can shiver with your
imaginary gods and art—
I'll sit and warm my feet
by my solid stone fireplace,
Ishiguro's *Artist of the Floating World*
still unread on the coffee table.

A cup of hot cocoa
might feel divine right now
but I don't get up to make it—
instead, as if guided by
some real god's hand, I pick up
a pen and begin to write—

first about a nude at a stove, then Ishiguro
and finally about stepping
over my sleeping dog on the way
to the kitchen to make hot cocoa
with whipped cream and marshmallows
floating on top.

In the Post-Hunting Era

I kick my dog
out of the house to go play
in the snow

Clouds run across
the sky like
gray pack animals

How sad if a wolf progeny
were to grow lame in front
of the fireplace

As the progeny of one thing
or another I almost get out of my chair
to join him

My Trip to Romania

After reading about the young boy born
without sweat glands who panted to keep cool
and in the same small town a beagle whose paws
perspired when nervous and forehead dripped
during the hot summer months

I felt a strange compulsion to fly to Romania to see this for myself.
I made arrangements to attend the scheduled meeting
between the boy and the dog that was open to medical researchers
even though I'm not in the medical field and my research
is mostly limited to comparing restaurant ratings on Yelp.

Upon arrival at the farmhouse where the dog resided
I nuzzled my way into the crowded living room
where I laid eyes on the hound who would appear quite ordinary
if not for the fact that he periodically wiped his dripping brow
with his paw while neatly stacking wooden ABC blocks.

When the boy arrived with his mother it was clear that
he and the dog had met before and enjoyed a close bond—
ignoring the researchers and reporters in the room the dog
yelped affectionately and stroked the boy's head with a damp paw
while the boy obsequiously licked the dog behind its ear.

Several gasps and utterances from observers were overheard
with certain words and phrases lingering in the air—transmutation,
reincarnation, what in tar nation—but I remained quiet, scratching
an itch on my left leg with my right leg, staring at the tennis ball
the boy chewed on determinedly.

Without air conditioning the crowded room soon became too hot
for the boy so his mother bade us goodbye and whisked him home.
I chatted with other observers for a while and then we departed.
As we walked down the long dirt driveway toward our rental cars
a plump brown rabbit darted out from behind a bush—

I tore off after it then abruptly froze, remembering
my circumstances. Feigning disinterest, I allowed
the rabbit to skitter away and tried to appear nonchalant
as I straightened my white shirt sleeves
and pulled at my too-tight collar.

Salute to Military Dogs

With a clipboard and box of dog biscuits
I hovered outside PetSmart polling
passing pooches on whether they'd
willingly join the military's K-9 Corps

and my tallied results showed that while 100 percent
wagged their tail when offered treats
zero percent said they'd enlist in the military regardless
of any opinions proffered by their people companions –

in fact zero percent said anything at all
which confirms to me that K-9s don't volunteer for war
but are instead dealt draft lottery numbers
with no exemptions for college or bone-spur-stricken paws

making it unthinkable to not let returning four-legged
troops up on the couch like our poodles and dachshunds
who still believe that the world's worst evil
is squirrels stealing seed from bird feeders.

The Harmonious Art of Tai Chi

While I treasure the slow, graceful
movements of tai chi for their health benefits
and meditative peace of mind

I'm particularly fond of the poetic names
for the postures performed in this ancient
and harmonious martial art—

Fair Lady Works the Shuttle, Grasping
the Sparrow's Tail, Wave Hands Like Clouds,
Parting the Wild Horse's Mane…

When you randomly accost me shouting
I'm Gonna Knock Your Fucking Teeth Out
I think not only have you missed out

on the non-confrontational spirit of tai chi,
but also the mellifluous metaphors
in the postures' names –

Fetching a Needle from the Sea Bottom
comes to mind as I envision bending down
over your limp body and feeling for a pulse

should you decide to follow me
when I walk away, a quiet but fearless
Tiger Returning to the Mountain.

Cover Letter to the Poetry Editor

Please consider the three enclosed poems—
"In the Throes of My Hip Throws,"
"Dizzied by Her Spinning Back Fists,"
and "Is He Dead or Just Knocked Out?"—
for publication in your esteemed quarterly.

From what I've read of the words and sentences
in your journal, I am confident your readers
will like these poems.

Now for my bio:
I leave it to you to deduce why this bio
doesn't reference any previously published poems,
but I will share an accolade I've received—
I was inducted into The United States Martial Arts Hall of Fame
in the category of Outstanding Kung Fu Master.
Many kung fu masters can spout aphorisms satisfactorily
but they can't fight. I am an excellent fighter, confident
that in a real fight I would defeat any of the world's
poets, even the strong ones in their 20s or 30s who box or wrestle
because what my overly-experienced body has lost
in speed and strength, my mind makes up for
with a heightened clarity and sharpness garnered
from decades of Zen meditation and several years of trying
to decipher the abstruse poems of modern hybridists.

As an editor you are surely aware that most
poetry submissions are just that—poetry submissions—
but I also intermix all the common grappling submissions
like arm bars and leg locks and the really painful
finger and toe locks that are banned in most tournaments
due to too many injuries but hey in street fights, like open
mic readings, anything goes.

I imagine that before you make a final decision
on whether to publish my poems you want to know
how I've fared in poetry contests—
I can share in all humility that as with fist fights, I've never
lost a single poetry contest. The Shaolin kung fu
I practice is rooted in Buddhism, which teaches
that all phenomena are temporary and illusory.
How can I have lost a poetry contest or a fist fight
when they aren't even real? All of my broken bones
and crappy poems and torn ligaments of the past
were mere illusions, though I do admit
that the concussions have taken a real toll.

In closing, I recognize that the bio section of this cover letter
is way too long for a busy editor whose submission guidelines
specify bios of twenty-five words or less
but I felt that all of this had to be said to give my poems
a fighting chance at publication and anyway
what are you going to do about it,
kick my ass?

My Mom, Earnest and Bright

When my yellow-bellied slider Earnest went missing
I looked frantically around my room
and double-checked under the rocks and plants
at the bottom of the clear plastic tank
that I'd custom built for him in my 7th grade shop class
earning me an A+ which I mention only in case
you assumed I'd built some flimsy-assed tank
that would invite a turtle's easy escape.

My mom cried and I cried as we looked
under the furniture in every room of the house
and soon even my dog Bright joined us
in our grieving with a sick and forlorn demeanor
that seemed to intensify right up until the moment
she vomited on the couch and we'd found Earnest.

Thirty years later as my mom lay confined to her bed
day after day and month after month
finally asking, *Why can't I die already*
I looked up into the night sky and asked Bright
if it was hunger or mercy that drove her to take Earnest
from the plastic tank I'd custom built
that I never realized kept him from wherever
he wanted to be.

Steeples

When I first heard the expression
I asked my mom if it's true
that even the pope wakes up with a hard-on
and she said no, he's too old.

Thus, among the old, I believed,
only steeples point to heaven.
Now I question why so many
clergymen cast their gazes upward

yet point their flesh
at the most innocent and vulnerable
—our children.
I ask my long-gone mom

if this sickness will ever end
and from the cosmos she replies
yes dear, when the earth grows old
and the toppled steeples

dangle in the wind.

Quieted

Last night my wife asked if I'd like
to have a fire in the fireplace
and I said no, I'd prefer to have a fire
in the clothes dryer.

This morning I awoke to learn
that on our quiet residential block
a young woman with her baby son
and elderly father were out taking a walk

when they were run over
by a teenage driver distracted by her phone
and only the baby survived
with injuries.

My wife asked if I'd like
to have a smoothie for breakfast
and I said no,
thank you.

Lingering Questions

Playing Twenty Questions with my grandma
I would ask, *Baba, is it bigger than a bread box?*
even though I had no clue how big a bread box was
in that new era of plastic bags and wonder breads.

I never thought to ask how she'd coped
when her father was shot and killed as he left their basement
and snuck out into the street to find a loaf of bread
to feed her and her brother.

A century has now passed since hunger and fear
forced my Baba and her brother to flee their home in Kyiv
and trek for weeks across the continent
to reach the coast and board a boat

to America, where grief might be balanced by hope.
We have declared that hope springs eternal perhaps
because we must—is there another option in a world
where war is eternal?

As children once again flee Kyiv, many leaving
fathers behind in plastic body bags, I wonder if it will be
hearts of hope or hearts of darkness that grow
bigger than a bread box.

Broken

An odd thing about
my dad
is in all the years I knew him
he never mentioned
a single thing about his childhood,
not even a word or two
about his own
mom or dad
growing up.

So at least now
I've broken one
family pattern.

Return to 42nd Street

42nd Street in the '70s and '80s was scattered
with sex-toy stores, peep shows, shadowy XXX movie
theaters, C-grade chopsocky cinemas and street corner

evangelists hollering at hookers and pushers
to find Jesus before the end arrives
or at me as I'd walk from my job on 2nd Avenue

to my subway stop at 8th Avenue, past marquees
that sucked me in to view hits like Master of the Flying
Guillotine or The 36th Chamber of Shaolin.

Once in a while I'd slip into the confessional-shaped
peep show booths where instead of dropping to your knees
you dropped coins into the slot

to watch porn goddesses drop to their knees and confess
their willingness to do anything and show everything
except personality

or I'd thumb through the racks of magazines
whose photo spreads made Playboy and Penthouse
seem like Sunday-school prayer books.

Last year I returned to 42nd Street for the first time
in thirty years to find the prostitutes and pushers
replaced by moms and dads from Iowa pushing

strollers with blond two-year-olds sporting
Mickey Mouse sunglasses, the sex shops and theaters
demolished to make way for chain restaurants

like Applebee's and Hard Rock Café. I hailed
a cab and left the neighborhood
as soon as possible.

When the Moon Shines Up from Between My Feet

that doesn't mean the natural order
has been shaken,
only that I've pissed
a large reflecting pool

or my sense of self
has grown so big
that I misperceive the moon
as beneath me.

I come back down
to earth
by reminding myself
that I can't touch the clouds

or cast light on moths
flittering from leaf to leaf
and I've never really pissed
a reflecting pool

only added my small stream
to existing ponds
that don't notice me
or not notice me

their placid waters
in the exact state
of being that I'm
seeking

The Death of My Friend

I've died a million deaths
so I'm used to it.

After each death a resurrection,
a chance at redemption

taken lightly. Will I ever put to rest
these nagging sensations,

the ones the sutras say
end upon awakening?

Master Joshu said after breakfast
go wash your bowl,

so much simpler
than anyone imagined.

I should call the funeral home
to report the death of my friend

but instead I call
for take-out

and in between bites my friend
and I laugh out loud

because of course a friend like self
doesn't die that easily.

Sitting in Meditation

during my morning yoga class I'm reminded
of Mr. Fiorini, my fifth-grade teacher
tasked with teaching us about human cells—

I'd raised my hand and asked whether
we grow bigger because our cells grow bigger
or because we grow more cells
and he asked, what kind of question is that?
I hadn't learned the categories of questions yet
so I shrugged my shoulders shyly
and he moved on.

No third eye opened but one eye
half open scanning the room
I observe the meditators around me—
most are middle-aged or beyond
with inert bodies appearing shrunken
and partially decomposed like
a still life painting of half-eaten fruit.
I glance down at my own arms
and find them much skinnier
and funnier looking than I remembered.

Having never received an answer I'm still not sure—
do we grow shorter in old age because our cells
get smaller, or because we have fewer cells?

I close my eye to resume my meditation
but it reopens and my gaze returns to the man
in black shorts seated across from me
who I see often in class with his chopstick legs
and toothpick arms and I wonder, what is it
about him today that has reminded me
so much of Mr. Fiorini, completely
ruining my meditation?

With Eager Anticipation

At poetry readings I sometimes notice
the poets' hands shake while holding
books or papers, perhaps from nerves
or too much excitement.

It's occurred to me that if their hands
are going to tremble like that anyway
they could do something more practical
than read poems aloud—

maybe stand behind the bar
and shake martinis at Applebee's
or help mix paint
at Home Depot.

Now whenever a bartender picks up
a cocktail shaker I lean forward
with eager anticipation,
listening for a coming poem.

I Would Have Left You Everything

In poetry my mind
is empty,
in meditation
full of poems.

With empty pockets turned
inside out, lenders turn me away.
When full, they pour me
chardonnay.

The harder I live,
the sooner I'll die.
The closer to death,
the more alive I feel.

How unlucky
for both of us
my life follows
this ironic pattern—

willing at last
to sign a final will
I can't find a pen anywhere
in this whole damned house.

The 5th of July

Finding a parking spot
right on Main Street
I set up my folding chair
beneath the cool shade of an oak tree
and enjoy the unobstructed view—

an old cat with a red collar ambling
along the street, a mother in white shorts
whose baby stares at me from its stroller
but doesn't wave, a bluebird pecking at dropped
popcorn as it warily watches the cat.

Ignoring prodding from friends and family
I stayed home yesterday, opting instead
for today's impromptu parade. I light a sparkler
and wave it in the quiet air, celebrating
my independence.

Acknowledgements

I wish to thank the following publications for including some of these poems in slightly different form:

Kakalak: "Hiding Something" (2017), "Mandarin Love Poem" (2017) and "Covenants" (2023)

Main Street Rag: "Cover Letter to the Poetry Editor" (2018)

Many thanks to my cousin, the talented artist Suzanne Sbarge, for allowing the use of her fine collage painting "Flight" on the cover of this book (suzannesbarge.com).

A special thanks to the great folks at Charlotte Center for Literary Arts, both for offering such a wide array of classes and events with nationally-renowned poets and authors, and for creating Charlotte Lit Press and accepting my manuscript for publication. I have particularly benefited from taking numerous Charlotte Lit courses with my friend and mentor Dannye Romine Powell and the late Anthony S. Abbott, and from the feedback received from Dannye and Stuart Dischell during a year-long Poetry Chapbook Lab. Additionally, the collaboration with many published poets and fine writers whom I have met through these courses has been invaluable.

Finally, I am indebted to Paul Reali and Kathie Collins, founders of Charlotte Center for Literary Arts, for their careful reading and editorial suggestions to improve this chapbook.

About the Author

Eric Sbarge grew up in Chicago and New York, then moved to Charlotte, North Carolina, in 1994 when his Taiwan-born wife Wan Chih (Debra) asked if they could find someplace warmer to live. In Charlotte they founded The Peaceful Dragon Tea House and Cultural Center, which grew into the largest school in the Carolinas for tai chi, kung fu, Zen meditation and related arts. Today they and their three wiener dogs split their time between Charlotte and their mountain home in Banner Elk, NC, and he continues to teach tai chi and kung fu, and write poetry.

www.ingramcontent.com/pod-product-compliance
Lightning Source LLC
Chambersburg PA
CBHW031300120626
46545CB00007B/2917